WORLD PRESS PHOTO 08

 Thames & Hudson

Contents

Chairman of the 2008 jury > **Gary Knight**

Standing in judgment over one's peers is a rather uncomfortable task, and not one that the jury of this year's World Press Photo awards took lightly. The judges made a deliberate decision to prioritize what we considered to be the best photography of an issue, rather than the issue itself. We felt qualified to judge the photography, but not to stand in judgment over the world — nor to decide whether disease was a more important issue than migration, poverty or homelessness.

One of the results of that decision is that many of the grave issues of our time do not appear on these pages, because the jury felt that they were not photographed well enough.

A principal purpose of the World Press Photo contest is to celebrate great achievements in press photography, and it is disappointing that so much of what was submitted was familiar. One wonders why some photojournalists spend time and energy telling us what we already know, in a style borrowed from another photographer. Certainly, many ongoing stories linger unresolved and should not be forgotten — but if they are going to be revisited, it is essential to create urgency, offer solutions, and not just to repeat what has been done before. One is left with the impression that many entries were submitted because they looked like previous winners' photos. Their sole purpose appeared to be to win prizes, a pointless journalistic exercise.

There is much to celebrate in this year's list of winners, not least of which is the usurping of some legends of the photojournalist establishment by youth. The fact that sixteen awards were made to former World Press Photo Joop Swart Masterclass students is testament to this fourteen-year-old program's success in identifying and nurturing tomorrow's great messengers.

This year's contest respectfully acknowledges photographers working in the great traditions of photojournalism but there is also a significant embracing of those who push to the limits what many will find comfortable, of work that challenges the conventions of what press photography has become, or could be.

The judges sought to reward creative, effective journalism and were excited by images that didn't offer simplistic solutions, but which did something more difficult — stimulated viewers' curiosity and raised questions in people's minds. This is as much about journalism as it is about photography, and in looking through this book the reader accepts a responsibility handed on by the photographers and the jury to learn. You are encouraged to pay attention to the captions and follow them up with thought and further research. We hope that after looking at these pictures, readers will understand a little better how the world works and our place in it. The book does not mark the end of a process but a new beginning.

Much of the work you will see in these pages, and in the exhibition that travels worldwide, represents the world in a way that many of us are unaccustomed to seeing it; in a way that throws down a challenge to the public to re-engage with the media. It is also a challenge to those of us in the media who may find these essays uncomfortably unorthodox. The future has arrived.

People in the News

SINGLES

1st Prize
Yonathan Weitzman

2nd Prize
Carol Guzy

3rd Prize
Daniel Berehulak

STORIES

1st Prize
Philippe Dudouit

2nd Prize
Francesco Zizola

3rd Prize
Oded Balilty

The dress of an African girl hangs on a barbed-wire fence after she has crossed the Israeli-Egyptian border with her family, on August 20. A growing number of migrants, many from the conflict-torn Darfur area of Sudan, passed illegally into Israel in 2007. Many had already lived for some years in Egypt. Israel argued that such people were not refugees but economic migrants, and further reserved the right to refuse entry to asylum-seekers from enemy countries, of which Sudan was regarded as one. In July, the Egyptian president had promised to step up action against border infiltrators, and the Egyptian military adopted a more aggressive stance towards people attempting illegal crossings.

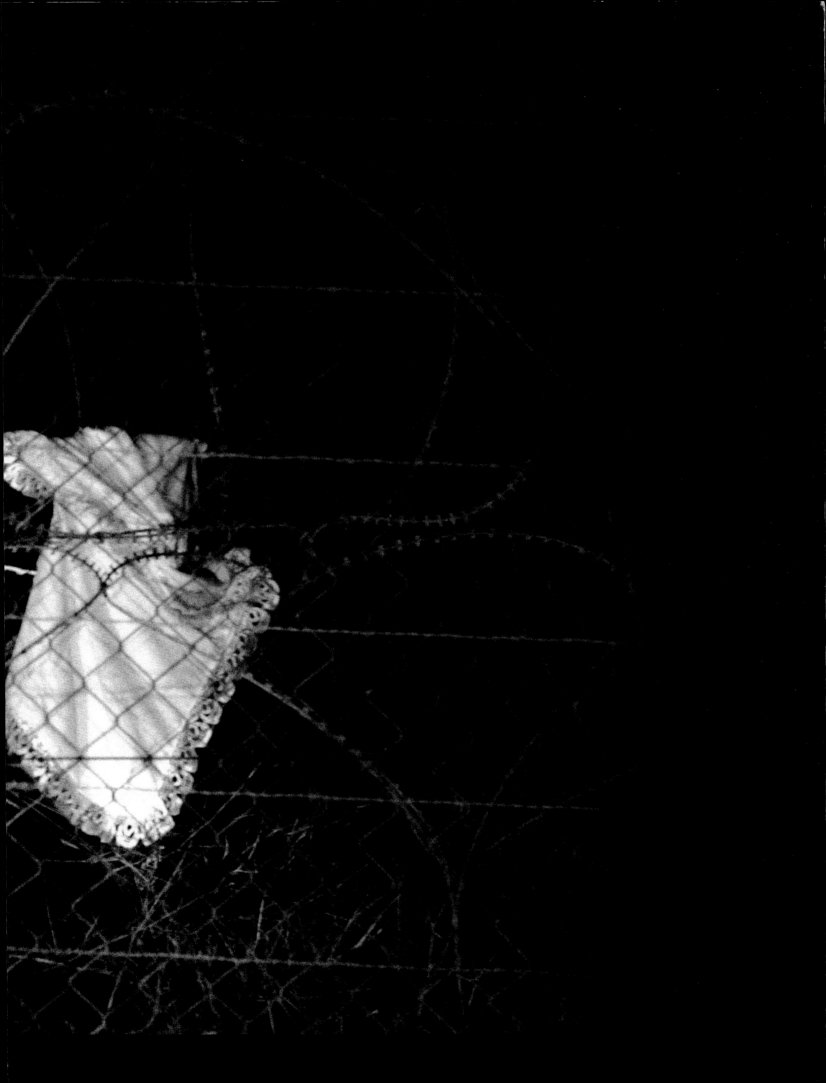

Conflict between Turkish authorities and militant fighters of the Kurdistan Workers' Party (PKK), who are calling for an independent Kurdish state, has lasted decades and cost more than 30,000 lives. More than half the world's Kurds (10 to 12 million people) live in the southeastern part of Turkey, near the border with Iraq. This page: PKK commander Haval Syavent stands in the forest near the PKK camp of Arbur in northern Iraq. Facing page: A PKK fighter near the Arbur camp. (continues)

(continued) Turkey, together with the USA and the European Union, has designated the PKK a terrorist organization. In 2007, Turkey accused the PKK of launching attacks from bases in the semi-autonomous Kurdish region of northern Iraq, and threatened cross-border retaliatory strikes. This page: Fighters undergo a training session at the PKK Women's Military School, in the province of Zap in northern Iraq.

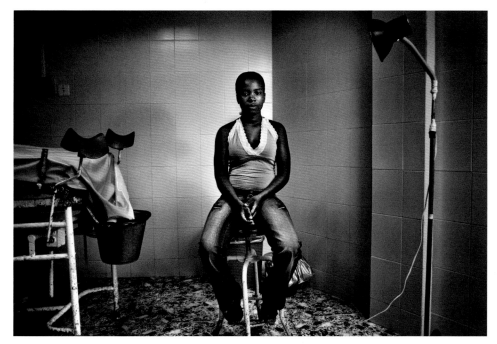

Violence has become endemic in Colombia, a country long ravaged by conflict involving national security forces, outlawed armed groups and drug cartels. Women are particularly affected as victims of sexual assault. Aid workers suspected of helping guerillas and marginal groups have also been targeted. Facing page: A 14-year-old victim of group sexual abuse waits in a clinic in Quibdo, western Colombia. This page, top: Martha (26) is a sex worker, as her mother was. Middle: Filomena (22) waits for an abortion, having twice been raped.

In December 1937, Japanese troops captured Nanjing, then the capital of China. A period of violence ensued, in what has become known as the Nanjing Massacre. As people gathered in Nanjing to commemorate the 70th anniversary of the event, there was still no agreement regarding the number of victims, the extent of atrocities committed, and the duration of the massacre. China maintains that some 300,000 people were killed, with thousands of others raped and tortured. Japan disputes the figures, saying the scale of killing and rape was considerably smaller. As the two countries become increasingly close trading partners, some effort is being made to avoid flaming antagonisms over what remains a delicate issue.

Left to right, from top: People read names of victims in the Nanjing Massacre Memorial Hall. People in Nanjing pay their respects at the ceremony commemorating the 70th anniversary of the massacre. Chinese paramilitary rehearse for the commemoration ceremony. A member of the Chinese paramilitary at the massacre memorial. Members of the Chinese paramilitary parade during the commemoration ceremony. An industrial area in Nanjing. People visit the monument to the massacre. Cheng Yun (88), a survivor of the massacre, stands outside his home in Nanjing.

People gather for a candlelight vigil for brothers Jeremy and Justin Herring, aged 18 and 20, found dead of gunshot wounds in their family home in Silver Spring, Maryland, USA. Their father, who was said by a relative to suffer from mental illness and depression, was charged with their murder.

Former Pakistani prime minister Benazir Bhutto adjusts her headscarf during a press conference at her house in Karachi on October 21. Bhutto had returned to Pakistan four days earlier after eight years of self-imposed exile, in order to lead her Pakistan People's Party in upcoming elections. A suicide bomb attack during her homecoming parade resulted in 139 fatalities. Bhutto held prayers for those killed in the bombing, blaming Islamist militants for their deaths. In a second attack, after a party rally on December 27, Benazir Bhutto was assassinated.

Spot News

SINGLES
1st Prize
John Moore
2nd Prize
Bold Hungwe
3rd Prize
Stephen Morrison
Honorable Mention
Emilio Morenatti
STORIES
1st Prize
John Moore
2nd Prize
Roberto Schmidt
3rd Prize
Mike Kamber

Two rockets are launched from Gaza City towards Israel on May 22. Seven missiles were fired by Palestinian militants that day, lightly wounding two people, the Israeli army reported. Israel responded with four air raids, targeting suspected arms caches and Hamas militant bases. Palestinian officials said seven people were wounded in the raids. A week earlier, Israel had resumed air strikes on Gaza after a six-month lull, in response to Hamas rocket attacks on Israeli towns. In June, the Palestinian government proposed a ceasefire.

After three American soldiers were captured in the Sunni stronghold of Latafiya, south of Baghdad, in May, some 4,000 US troops and 2,000 Iraqi soldiers mounted a search operation. As patrols fanned out to search the countryside, they were hindered by IEDs ('improvised explosive devices') buried far from roads. Left: A soldier is killed and three wounded after one of them steps on an IED. Right: Soldiers load dead and wounded comrades onto a medivac helicopter.

Supporters of Zimbabwe's main opposition party, the Movement for Democratic Change (MDC), run from water-cannon blasts and tear gas after police barred them from attending a rally in the capital Harare, on February 18. Leader of the party Morgan Tsvangirai had planned to use the gathering to launch a campaign for the presidency. The MDC obtained a court ruling allowing them to hold the event, but police ignored the decision. Tension was high in Zimbabwe, where inflation was running at 1,600 percent and unemployment at 70 percent, after President Robert Mugabe announced plans to defer presidential elections.

Kenyan policemen chase protestors during unrest and looting in the opposition stronghold of Kibera, in Nairobi, after disputed presidential elections in December. Thousands of people took to the streets after incumbent president Mwai Kibaki claimed victory and a second term in office. According to official results, the president won by just 230,000 votes out of a total ballot of nearly 10 million. Opposition candidate Raila Odinga said the elections had been rigged, and prepared to declare himself head of state. Protests and ethnic clashes between President Kibaki's Kikuyu community and Luo opposition supporters led to hundreds of deaths nationwide and some 250,000 people being displaced.

Unrest swept through Kenya after people disputed current leader Mwai Kibaki's narrow victory in presidential elections. The European Union observer mission backed opposition claims that some vote figures had been inflated. There were accusations of suspicious delays in announcing results, and of tampering with the electoral register. This page: People stampede down a street in Kibera, Nairobi, after hearing shots fired in the vicinity. Protestors had been ransacking stores and setting fire to property. Facing page, top: A supporter of defeated candidate Raila Odinga waves a stick during protests in Kibera, an opposition stronghold. Below: Eighty-year-old Thabita carries her cat, the only possession she was able to salvage when her home was burned down in Mathare, Nairobi.

Pakistan opposition leader Benazir Bhutto was assassinated after addressing thousands of supporters at a rally in the city of Rawalpindi, on December 27. She had been campaigning ahead of general elections scheduled for January. As Bhutto's convoy was leaving the rally, an attacker opened fire on her car. Shortly after that a bomb exploded. No autopsy was carried out on the former prime minister, and it was unclear as to whether she had died from bullet wounds, from the explosion, or by hitting her head on the sunroof as she ducked back into her car. This page: Benazir Bhutto addresses supporters at Liaqat Bagh Park in Rawalpindi. Facing page, top: Bhutto waves from the escape hatch of her armored vehicle, seconds before being assassinated. Below: A bomb explodes next to the former prime minister's vehicle. (continues)

(continued) At least 20 other people died in the bomb blast. Bhutto's assassination sparked days of nationwide rioting, and raised the question of whether elections would be postponed. Supporters claimed that government security provisions for the opposition leader, who had recently returned to Pakistan from exile, had been inadequate. Facing page, top: A survivor grieves at the site of the attack, just minutes after Bhutto's assassination. Below: A poster of Benazir Bhutto lies beside bomb-blast victims, who are covered with flags of her Pakistan People's Party. This page: A survivor is overcome with emotion at the site of the assassination attack. Next page: The moment of the blast.

General News

SINGLES
1st Prize
Balazs Gardi
2nd Prize
Stanley Greene
3rd Prize
Takagi Tadatomo
Honorable Mention
Christoph Bangert
STORIES
1st Prize
Balazs Gardi
2nd Prize
Tim Hetherington
3rd Prize
Cédric Gerbehaye

The victim of an attack by members of the Mungiki gang lies in a street in downtown Nairobi. Mungiki began as a secretive sect in Kenya in the 1980s, espousing a return to traditional values and a rejection of Western beliefs. Members were known for their trademark dreadlocks and rituals of tobacco sniffing. Banned in 2002, the sect appears to have evolved over the years into an underworld gang involved in murder, extreme violence, extortion and racketeering. Its activities are said to include demanding protection money from minibus taxi drivers and levying heavy fees for water and electricity supply in slum areas.

A sketch in the sand illustrates an assault on Furawiya village in Darfur in western Sudan in 2003. The diagram was drawn four years later in January 2007, in a refugee camp in neighboring Chad by Asdallah Asdel Khaled, a survivor of the attack. He had witnessed the total destruction of his village, and atrocities committed against its inhabitants. Between 2003 and 2007, over 200,000 people were killed and 2.5 million displaced by ethnic conflict in Darfur, with large numbers fleeing to Chad.

A man holds a wounded boy in front of a house in the village of Yaka China, in the Korengal Valley in northeastern Afghanistan. The boy received shrapnel wounds from a rocket during a US air strike on a suspected insurgent position in the village. Korengalis have a reputation for being tough and clannish, and have fought off all outside attempts to control them – including that of the Taliban in the 1990s. After the strike, which villagers said killed and wounded a number of civilians, elders declared jihad on American forces in the valley.

In October, combined American and Afghan National Army forces conducted Operation Rock Avalanche to flush out insurgents from the Korengal Valley and surrounding areas of northeastern Afghanistan. The Korengal Valley is considered to be the epicenter of US fighting in Afghanistan, and one of the deadliest zones of conflict in the region. Located near the Pakistan border, it was the first part of a former mujahideen smuggling channel, used to bring men and arms into the country. American military strategists believed that al-Qaeda was trying to revive the route. Above: Men are made to stand at a distance from each other as US soldiers search their village. (continues)

Nearly three-quarters of all bombs dropped by NATO forces in Afghanistan are dropped on and around the Korengal Valley. Yet much of the fighting is on foot, and ground gained is measured in yards, single hilltops, small patches of forest. Previous spread, clockwise from top left: A soldier checks a thermal imaging machine near Kop, the main US base in the valley. Soldiers drag an injured comrade to shelter under fire. A doctor treats an injured soldier while under attack. A mortar company returns fire from the Kop base. Facing page, top: US forces bomb an insurgent position with phosphorus. Below: A US helicopter lands in Yaka China to pick up an American commander, after a meeting in the wake of US bombing of the village. This page, top: A wounded child is carried from a house in Yaka China, following the US air strike targeting insurgents in the village.

A German Army target for sniper practice is set up in Kunduz, Afghanistan. Some 3,200 German troops are in Afghanistan as part of the NATO-led International Security Assistance Force (ISAF) – the first time since World War II that the army has been deployed outside Germany. Based mainly in northern Afghanistan and around the capital Kabul, the troops are primarily involved in reconstruction work.

Contemporary Issues

SINGLES

1st Prize
Brent Stirton

2nd Prize
Zsolt Szigetváry

3rd Prize
William Daniels

STORIES

1st Prize
Jean Revillard

2nd Prize
Lorena Ros

3rd Prize
Olivier Culmann

Five years after the closure of the Sangatte refugee center near Calais, some 500 migrants sleep rough in makeshift shelters on the city outskirts. Many have fled conflict in Iraq, Afghanistan and Darfur, and are hoping to stow away in trains or vehicles heading through the Channel tunnel to seek asylum in the UK. In April, the mayor of Calais announced plans to build some basic facilities for migrants on an abandoned football pitch.

The last available study, conducted in 1994, indicated that 23 percent of girls and 15 percent of boys under the age of 17 in Spain had been sexually abused. Most abused children will never speak of their experience. These adult survivors believe that disclosing their personal stories will contribute to the prevention of future child sex abuse.

Facing page, top: Sara (21), Barcelona, was six when she complained that someone close to the family was interfering with her, but it wasn't until she was ten that she was heard. Below: Bartomeu (38) was sexually abused at the age of ten by a man who played football with him and his friends after school, in San Boi, Barcelona. He never spoke about it, until telling his wife 28 years later. This page, top: Jose (23) was abused by the neighborhood librarian in the library's lavatory, in El Prat, Barcelona, when he was 13. His abuser showered him with gifts and money. Jose's mother found out when he was 16, pressed charges, and the librarian was sentenced to seven years in prison. Below: Irene (22) is unsure at what age she was first subjected to incest, but it certainly started when she was a small child in Barcelona city. Only when she left home, at the age of 19, did she feel strong enough to confront her abuser.

A couple targeted in anti-gay violence after the Gay Pride parade in July, in Budapest, Hungary, wait for medical help. Later in the year, the Hungarian parliament passed legislation to give same-sex partners many of the same rights as married couples. But after decades under communist rule, when homosexuality in Eastern Europe was either banned or ignored, it is far less accepted than in Western Europe. For the first time in twelve years, the July gay rights parade in Budapest saw attacks on the participants. Many of the incidents involved neo-Nazi groups, and some commentators maintained this was part of an increase of intolerance towards minority groups in Hungary.

Daily Life

74 Da   76 Daily Life > **Benjamin Lowy** > USA, VII Network > 2nd Prize Singles

A Kabul marketplace, six years after the US-led invasion of Afghanistan and the fall of the Taliban regime.

Around 180,000 Palestinians, some 24,000 of them Christians, live in and around Bethlehem, nowadays part of the Palestinian territories. Also present are a number of Jewish settlements, with a population approaching 80,000. Left to right, from top: A motorist refuels beside the Israeli security wall near Rachel's Tomb, one of Judaism's most holy sites, just outside Bethlehem. Children play in the hills overlooking the city. Palestinian day-workers crowd into a corral in order to pass through a check point to Jerusalem – a process that can take up to two hours. Rochama Bedein shows off her smart frock before Passover dinner at her home in the Efrat settlement, between Bethle-hem and Hebron. Families gather in the Efrat settlement at an event to benefit a foundation set up in the memory of two Jewish teenagers, who were killed by Palestinian militants in a cave near Jerusalem in 2001. The Duheisha refugee camp occupies 1.5 square kilometers just south of Bethlehem, and is home to 10,000 people. Christian cousins Thomas and Bajd Barham dance at the Cosmos discotheque every Saturday night, in the Christian town of Beit Jala, in the west of Bethlehem. Abu Majed and his family work on their farm, which has been divided in two by the Israeli security wall (which can be seen in the background), near the Efrat settlement.

Torez, in southeastern Ukraine, was once a flourishing coal mining town. Under communism, miners' salaries were among the highest in the Soviet Union, and miners were seen as national heroes. But since Ukrainian independence, the coal industry has attracted little government investment, becoming unprofitable and inefficient. With many mines in disrepair, safety has become an issue. The mines at Torez are deep, and extraction costly. Scores of them have been closed, leaving many miners jobless. Facing page, top: Workers leave Progress, the largest mine in the area, also threatened with closure. Below: Students skip classes to hang out at the entrance to a store. This page: Pensioner friends walk home after a birthday party in their neighborhood.

Portraits

Vladimir Putin, President of the Russian Federation

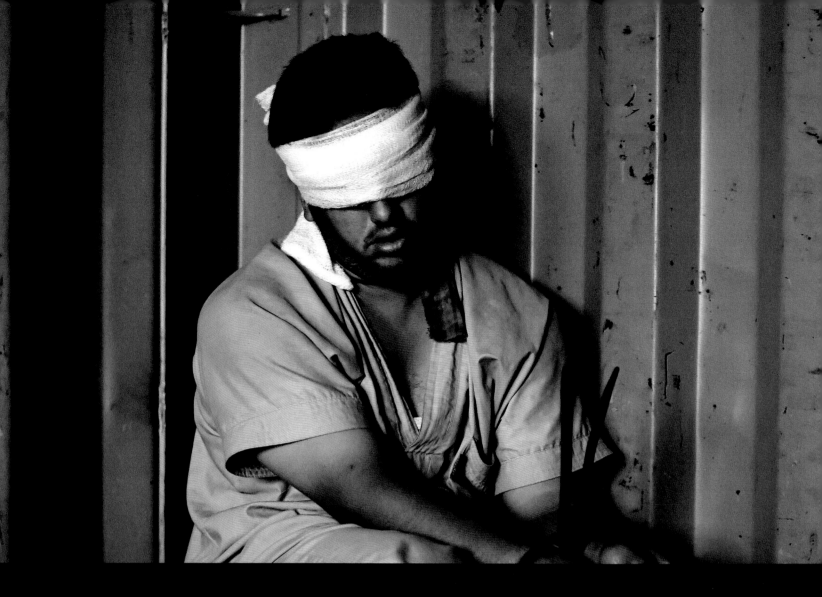

Iraqi detainees await transportation to a prison facility after American and Iraqi forces arrested them on suspicion of insurgent activity, in Arab Jabour, south of Baghdad, in August.

Arts and Entertainment

SINGLES

1st Prize

Ariana Lindquist

2nd Prize

Stefano De Luigi

3rd Prize

Qi Xiaolong

STORIES

1st Prize

Rafal Milach

2nd Prize

Massimo Siragusa

3rd Prize

Cristina García Rodero

A Shanghai girl waits backstage during a *cosplay* competition. Cosplay, a contraction of the English words 'costume' and 'play', began as a Japanese subculture in which people dressed as characters from *manga* comics, *anime* (animated films) or video games. Television shows, action films and pop music bands are also sometimes sources of inspiration. The pastime has become a worldwide phenomenon, with a growing following in mainland China.

Leisure parks in Italy give a more commercial atmosphere to what was traditionally simply a family excursion to the country or seaside. This page: Hot-air balloons float over the main entrance to Mirabilandia, in Ravenna. Covering some 750,000 square meters, it is one of the largest leisure parks in the country. Facing page: Visitors amuse themselves at 'El Castillo' water attraction at Mirabilandia. (continues)

(continued) Visitors swim in the Blue Lake water attraction, part of Italy's biggest water park, Aqua Paradise at Canevaworld, Lake Garda.

Actress Martina Gusmán on
the set of the film *Leonera*.
Gusmán is also a prominent
Argentine film producer. The
film was directed by Pablo
Trapero, a leading exponent of
nuevo cine argentino, which
arose in the 1990s. The
movement is known for films
portraying ordinary people in
everyday situations, in a
realistic quasi-documentary
style, usually with an element
of social criticism.

A storyteller entertains his audience in a teahouse in Tianjin, China. The ancient art of storytelling was labeled as reactionary after the 1949 communist revolution in China, and suppressed. In recent years it has seen a revival, with new teahouses — a traditional venue for listening to the myths and old tales — opening across the country. Storytellers perform in stylized, high-pitched voices, illustrating their narratives with gesture, and often accompanied by musical instruments.

Since the 1990s, circus has been in a decline. Poland's famous Julinek circus school has closed due to financial problems.

Retired circus artiste Jozef Maksymiuk (59), at home dressed in one of his old costumes.

The folk religion of María Lionza has one of the largest followings of any sect in Venezuela. The cult is a blend of African, indigenous and Roman Catholic beliefs, and is popular across all strata of Venezuelan society. María Lionza is revered as a goddess of nature, love, peace, and harmony. Various legends surround her origins, but followers believe she still lives on the mountain of Sorte, together with many other important spirits. Devotees travel to the mountain to pay homage to her and to commune with the spirit world. Left to right, from top: A woman undergoes a ritual cure as an alternative to surgery. People lie on beds of chalk as part of the healing process. Two men exchange energies — dress is kept to a minimum in the cult, as clothing is seen as a barrier to the spirits. A woman has candles placed in her mouth as a cure for madness. Violent mimicry is a characteristic of many rituals, but nobody gets hurt. An old woman lies in a pool of water — an important element in spiritual cleansing and a symbol of the cult's closeness to nature. A young man is covered in earth to help exorcise bad spirits.

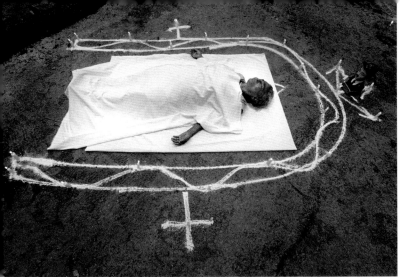

Nature

SINGLES
1st Prize
Fang Qianhua
2nd Prize
Jeff Hutchens
3rd Prize
Damon Winter
STORIES
1st Prize
David Liittschwager
2nd Prize
Paul Nicklen
3rd Prize
Paul Nicklen

A polar bear lies sedated on the ice near Kaktovik, above the Arctic Circle in Alaska. It had been shot with a tranquillizer dart by a United States Geological Survey scientist, researching the health of polar bear populations worldwide. As fears of global warming mount, and the bears' habitat appears increasingly threatened, scientists are debating whether preemptively to include them on the endangered list.

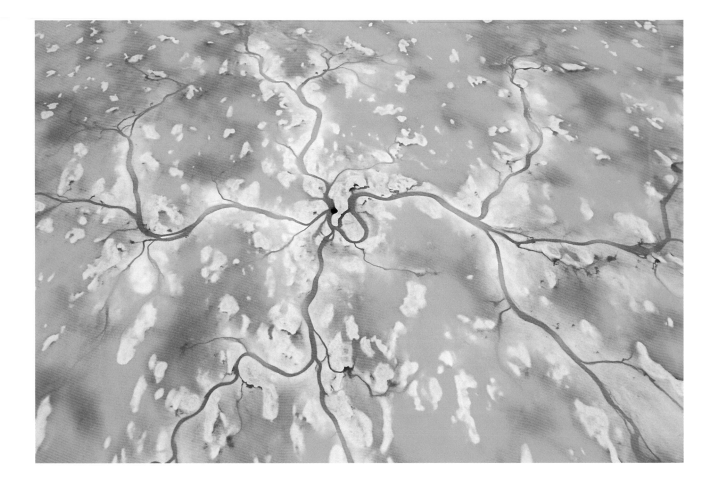

Ice is the very essence of the ecosystem of the Arctic. Sea ice — frozen seawater that moves with the ocean currents — provides an important habitat and resting place. Polar bears hunt and roam on the ice; seals rest and give birth there. Bowhead whales, which can live for up to 200 years, feed on minute creatures such as amphipods, which live out most of their lifecycle on the submerged surface of ice. Other whales feed on larger fish that hide as larvae in thin channels of ice. In recent years, satellite pictures have shown a dramatic reduction in Arctic ice cover. In 2007, sea ice reached a record low, a month before the end of the melt season. The situation, which many attribute to global warming, is compounded by the fact that water absorbs more solar rays than ice, and so speeds the thaw.

The moon rises over the Brooks Mountain Range in northern Alaska. To the north of these mountains, in the Beaufort Sea, proposed oil exploration threatens the subsistence way of life of the Inupiat people — Inuit communities living along the arid coastline. By some estimates, the oil off the Alaskan seabed could exceed all remaining reserves in the USA, but the Inupiat say that noisy drilling would affect whales' migration routes. The culture, traditions, and livelihoods of the Inupiat are centered on whaling and other seasonal hunting.

Sports Features

SINGLES
1st Prize
Andrew Quilty
2nd Prize
Miguel Riopa
3rd Prize
**Tomasz Gudzowaty
& Judit Berekai**
STORIES
1st Prize
Erik Refner

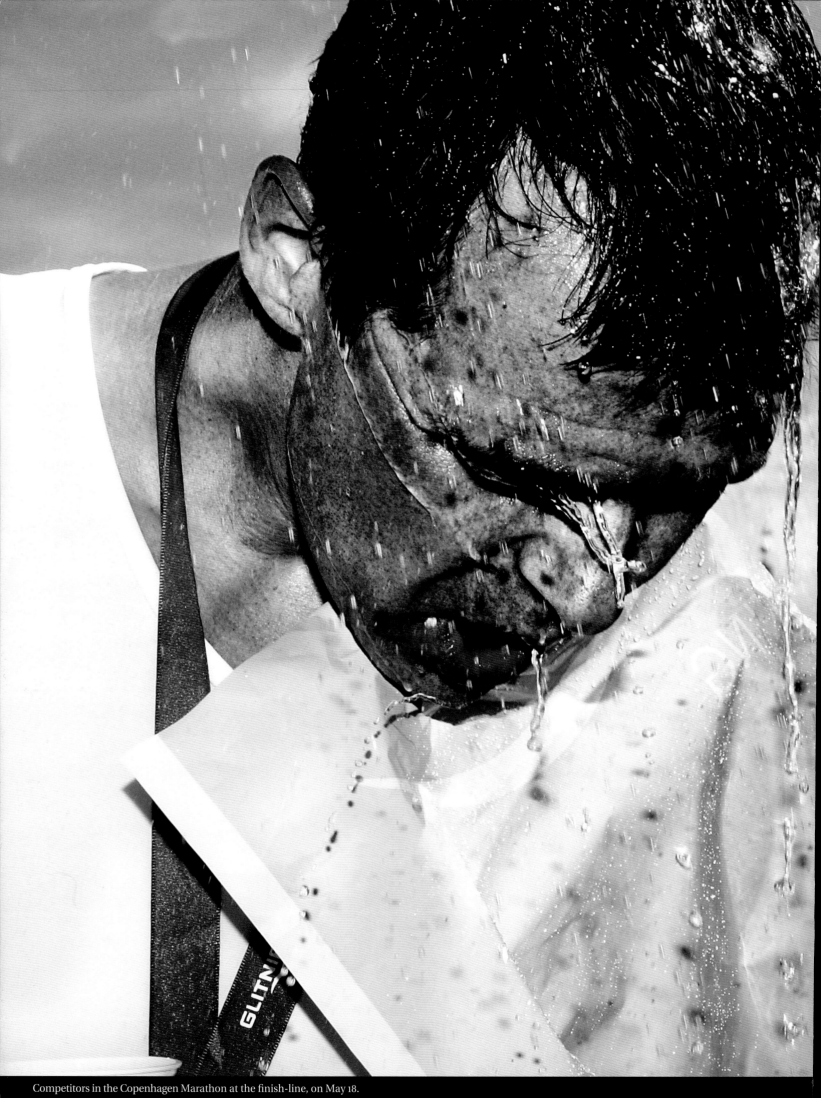

Competitors in the Copenhagen Marathon at the finish-line, on May 18.

In some states across the USA it is legal for children under the age of 12 to hunt if in the company of a licensed adult hunter. Approved prey includes wild turkeys and other birds, rabbits and small mammals, and stags of a certain height. The elimination of age barriers in hunting follows campaigns by some outdoor organizations to create earlier opportunities for youths to discover alternative recreational pursuits to computer games.

The 88-acre farm of Skatopia, near the tiny town of Rutland in rural Ohio, attracts skateboarders from all over the USA. A culture of anti-establishment behavior that surrounds skateboarding has made it difficult to integrate the sport into mainstream society. Founder Brewce Martin set up Skatopia not only as a large-scale skateboarding venue, but as a sanctuary for the sport's unconventional enthusiasts. People filter in and out at will. Some camp out for a day or two, others build cabins from scraps and stay for months.

Yoga practitioners exercise in the city of Varanasi, India. Formerly known as Benares, Varanasi is
one of the oldest cities in the world, and has long been a center for the study and practice of yoga.
A balance of physical exercise, breathing technique and *mudra* (gesture), yoga aims at a harmonizing
of body, mind and emotions.

Sports Action

SINGLES
1st Prize
Ivaylo Velev
2nd Prize
Frank Wechsel
3rd Prize
Miguel Barreira
STORIES
1st Prize
Tim Clayton
2nd Prize
Fei Maohua
3rd Prize
Chris Detrick

140 Sports Action > **Miguel Barreira** > Portugal, Record > 3rd Prize Singles

Bodyboarder Jaime Jesus competes in the Nazaré Special Edition championship at Praia do Norte, Nazaré, Portugal on December 16. The contest, one of the most important in Portuguese bodyboarding, does not begin until the waves are over three meters high. Jesus was tackling five-meter waves, and won the prize for the biggest wipe out (spectacular fall) during the competition.

Swiss professional freeride skier Phil Meier escapes an oncoming avalanche in Flaine, France, during Freeride Quest, a qualifying event for Xtreme Verbier, the freeriding world championship. The sport involves off-piste skiing through a variety of terrains, with very few restricting rules. It is not uncommon that a freerider triggers an avalanche. Meier finished the session safely. Of the 19 men competing in the event, five qualified for the world championships.

Swimmers pass the 250-meter buoy during a men's heat in the Triathlon World Cup in Rhodes, Greece, in October. The event comprises a 1.5-kilometer swim, a 40-kilometer bicycle ride and a 10-kilometer run.

Sports portfolio. This page: The Chinese synchronized swimming team practices on land during a training session for the FINA World Swimming Championships, which took place in Melbourne, Australia, in March. Facing page: Zhang Hongwei competes in the men's triple jump, after a heavy rain shower at the Seventh National Games for the Disabled, in Kunming, China on May 18. A world record-holder in this jump, Zhang came second in the event.

Sports Portfolio. This page: Pepperdine's Jason Walberg gouges the eyes of Brigham Young University's Jonathan Tavernari during a basketball match in Provo, Utah, USA. No foul was called. Although Tavernari missed the basket immediately after the incident, he was not injured. Later in the game he scored back-to-back three-pointers, helping his team win 86-67. Facing page: Cody Williams (17) falls off his unicycle after attempting a rock jump on the Slick Rock trail in Moab, Utah, USA, during the eighth annual Mountain Uni-cycling Festival. The March event attracted over 175 participants from across the world. Williams was not hurt.

TNT Global Express, Logistics & Mail

First published in the United Kingdom in 2008 by
Thames & Hudson Ltd, 181A High Holborn,
London WC1V 7QX

www.thamesandhudson.com

Published in 2008 in paperback in the United
States of America by Thames & Hudson Inc.,
500 Fifth Avenue, New York, New York 10110

www.thamesandhudsonusa.com

Art director
Teun van der Heijden
Advisors
Stephen Mayes
Bas Vroege
Design
Heijdens Karwei
Production coordinator
Virginie Baggen
Picture coordinators
Wiebke Duchow
Elsbeth Schouten
Nina Steinke
Captions & Interview
Rodney Bolt
Editorial coordinator
Erik de Kruijf
Editor
Kari Lundelin

Lithography
Wim Schoenmaker
Maurice Tromp
Kleurgamma Photolab, Amsterdam,
The Netherlands, www.kleurgamma.com

Paper
BVS 150 g/m², cover 300 g/m²
Papierfabrik Scheufelen GmbH, Lenningen,
Germany, www.scheufelen.com
Printing and binding
Wachter GmbH, Bönnigheim, Germany,
www.wachter.de
Production supervisor
Maarten Schilt
Mets & Schilt Publishers, Amsterdam,
The Netherlands, www.metsenschilt.com

This book has been published under the auspices
of Stichting World Press Photo, Amsterdam, The
Netherlands.

British Library Cataloguing-in-Publication Data:
A catalogue record for this book is available from
the British Library

ISBN 978-0-500-97677-7

Printed in Germany

Cover photograph
Tim Hetherington, UK, for Vanity Fair
*American soldier resting at bunker, Korengal Valley,
Afghanistan, 16 September*
World Press Photo of the Year 2007

Back cover photograph
Brent Stirton, South Africa, Reportage by Getty
Images for Newsweek
*Evacuation of dead mountain gorillas, Virunga
National Park, Eastern Congo*

About World Press Photo

World Press Photo is an independent nonprofit organization, founded in the Netherlands in 1955. Its
main aim is to internationally support and promote the work of professional press photographers.

Each year, World Press Photo invites press photographers throughout the world to participate in the
World Press Photo Contest, the premier annual international competition in press photography. All
photographs were judged in February 2008 in Amsterdam by an independent international jury
composed of thirteen professionals recognized in the field of press photography.

Educational projects play an important role in World Press Photo's activities. The annual Joop Swart
Masterclass is aimed at talented photographers at the start of their careers, and seminars and
workshops open to individual photographers, photo agencies and picture editors are organized in
developing countries.

For more information on World Press Photo, about the prizewinning images the photographers and for
an updated exhibition schedule, please visit: www.worldpressphoto.org

beauty delivered by TNT

For many people tulips are the symbol of Holland. Many bulbs
are transported by TNT, they bring joy to people across the globe.